Prehistoric Creatures Then and Now

TYRANNOSAURUS REx

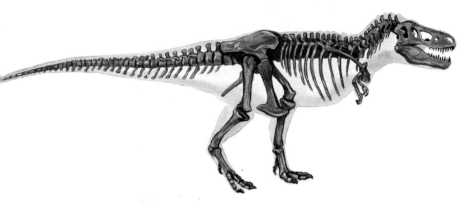

By K.S. Rodriguez
Illustrated by Patrick O'Brien

Steadwell Books

Raintree Steck-Vaughn Publishers
A Harcourt Company

Austin · New York
www.steck-vaughn.com

For William Arthur Squires, with love
Special thanks to Paul Marsh, Paleontology Researcher,
American Museum of Natural History

Produced by By George Productions, Inc.

Published by Raintree Steck-Vaughn Publishers,
an imprint of Steck-Vaughn Company

Library of Congress Cataloging-in-Publication Data
Rodriguez, K.S.
      Tyrannosaurus rex / by K.S. Rodriguez
          p.   cm — (Prehistoric creatures then and now)
      Summary: Introduces the Tyrannosaurus rex, describing its
characteristics, habitat, and behavior. Includes index.
      ISBN 0-7398-0104-X
      Tyrannosaurus rex — Juvenile literature. [1. Tyrannosaurus rex.
2 Dinosaurs.]   I. Title. II. Series.
QE862.S3 R56   2000
567.912'9 — dc21   99-053789

Printed and bound in the United States of America
10 9 8 7 6 5 4 3 2 1 LB 02 01 00 99

Photo Acknowledgments:
Pages 8, 22: Department of Library Services, American Museum of
Natural History; Page 21: Museum of the Rockies, Bruce Selyem;
Pages 26-27: Royal Tyrrell Museum of Paleontology/Alberta
Community Development.

Contents

King of the Dinosaurs

Picture a creature fiercer than a lion and hungrier than a shark. Picture a beast three times as tall as a grown person and about 50 feet (15 m) long—as long as an 18-wheel truck. Its sharp teeth can snap through a tree trunk. Its tail can knock down most other creatures with one blow.

This creature might sound like a make-believe monster. But it is not. Millions and millions of years ago, this giant lived on Earth. It was called Tyrannosaurus rex, king of the dinosaurs.

Tyrannosaurus rex was one of the largest dinosaurs that ever lived. ➤

Dinosaurs lived about 245 million to 65 million years ago. This was long before the first humans lived. The name dinosaur means "terrible large lizard." Dinosaurs were reptiles that lived on land and laid eggs.

Time line

Mesozoic
(The era of the dinosaurs)

prosauropod

Stegosaurus

Tyrannosaurus rex

Triassic	**Jurassic**	**Cretaceous**
245 million to 208 million years ago	208 million to 145 million years ago	145 million to 65 million years ago

Some dinosaurs were gentle plant eaters. Others, like Tyrannosaurus rex, were meat eaters. Some dinosaurs were as small as chickens. Others were bigger than trucks. Tyrannosaurus rex was one of the largest dinosaurs that ever lived.

Cenozoic
(The era of mammals, including humans)

mammoth

human

Tertiary
65 million to
5 million
years ago

Quaternary
1.6 million
years ago
to today

7

The Last of the Dinosaurs

The Age
of Mammals

Talk About Tyrannosaurus

Tyrannosaurus rex lived in what is now called North America some 85 million to 65 million years ago. This time was called the Cretaceous period.

Tyrannosaurus rex had a very powerful neck and jaw. ▼

◄ **A Tyrannosaurus rex skeleton in a museum**

Tyrannosaurus means "tyrant lizard." Rex means "king." Tyrannosaurus rex was thought to be the king of the dinosaurs because of its huge size and fierceness.

Tyrannosaurus rex could be 20 feet (6 m) tall. It weighed 6 tons—more than a truck. It had to eat that weight of meat every week just to live. That was not much of a problem for Tyrannosaurus rex. It could eat up to 500 pounds (230 kg) in one bite. This dinosaur could hunt and eat a 5-ton Triceratops for one meal. Or it could eat dinosaurs such as Hadrosaurus, Saltasaurus, Ankylosaurus, and Edmontosaurus. (Drawings of these dinosaurs are on page 29.) Its jaws were so big that it could eat smaller dinosaurs whole.

The sharp claws on Tyrannosaurus rex's feet could tear through the skin of a Triceratops.

Tyrannosaurus rex had very sharp teeth.

Tyrannosaurus rex's giant head was bigger than you are. Its eyes faced forward, so it could spot animals easily. Its jaws were the most powerful of any predator ever. A predator hunts and kills other animals. Tyrannosaurus rex's mouth was filled with 60 sharp teeth. They were as long as big knives. They could cut through the tough skin and hard bones of other dinosaurs.

Its heavy tail could knock down even the biggest dinosaurs. And the three sharp claws on its feet could hold them.

Tyrannosaurus rex was the fiercest predator of its time. Experts think that Tyrannosaurus rexes might have fought with each other for food.

Tyrannosaurus rex needed to eat 6 tons of meat every week.

13

Scientists aren't sure what Tyrannosaurus rex's small arms were used for.

Unsolved Mysteries

There are still many questions about dinosaurs. Scientists know that Tyrannosaurus rex was a deadly meat eater. Yet its arms were too short to reach its mouth, so they could not help it eat. Tyrannosaurus rex probably had to lower its head to the ground to eat. Its arms were also too weak to help Tyrannosaurus rex fight enemies or capture them.

What were the arms for? Tyrannosaurus rex may have used them to help it get up after sleeping. The two claws on its hands could grab the earth. Then the dinosaur could push itself up on its strong legs.

Scientists also wonder how fast Tyrannosaurus rex could run. Some experts think its legs were too heavy to let it run quickly. Others think Tyrannosaurus rex could run quickly but only for a short time.

How fast Tyrannosaurus rex could run also brings up another question. If the creature was slow, some experts think it could not have caught any prey. Prey are living creatures that are caught and eaten. Experts think perhaps it was a scavenger. This means it ate the meat of animals that were already dead.

Most experts think Tyrannosaurus rex had no problem hunting and catching prey. But some people think the creature could not have seen prey. This was because its eyes were so small.

Experts don't know if Tyrannosaurus rex hunted in packs or alone.

16

Scientists know that Tyrannosaurus rex laid eggs. They have found them in nests dug in the ground. But they are not sure how many eggs Tyrannosaurus rex laid at one time. Also, they do not know how this dinosaur cared for its eggs or its young.

What we know about dinosaurs is always changing. For many years scientists believed that Tyrannosaurus rex stood up straight and kept its heavy tail on the ground. They thought it may have used the tail to hold itself up. Now scientists think Tyrannosaurus rex leaned forward and held its tail up. Its tail might have helped it balance its huge head.

Because of this new theory, or idea, the famous Tyrannosaurus rex skeleton at the American Museum of Natural History in New York City was taken apart. Then it was put back together differently!

Triceratops and Tyrannosaurus rex may have lived near each other.

Digging for the Truth

How do we know anything about these animals from long ago? It is mostly thanks to scientists called paleontologists.

Paleontologists study clues called fossils. Fossils are remains of life long ago. A fossil can be a print of a plant or an animal.

A fossil can be a dinosaur bone. Or it can be a footprint. It can even be the mark of a bone—or body—left in a rock.

Some paleontologists study dinosaur fossils to learn more about these animals. They want to find out how these creatures looked and lived. They are like dinosaur detectives.

A paleontologist studies a fossil of Tyrannosaurus rex.

20

Barnum Brown was one of the world's most famous paleontologists. He was born in Kansas in 1873. As a child he liked to hunt on farms for fossils.

Brown found his first dinosaur fossil when he was 22 years old. It was the head of a Triceratops. Two years later he joined the staff of the American Museum of Natural History in New York City.

Barnum Brown
(1873 – 1963)

22

During his first year at the museum, he found an 86-foot (26-m)-tall Apatosaurus. It became the museum's first dinosaur.

Brown discovered the first Tyrannosaurus rex fossil in 1902. During his 66 years at the museum, Brown found many other dinosaur skeletons. These include Ankylosaurus, Allosaurus, and Diplodocus.

Brown's skill at finding fossils earned him the nickname "Mr. Bones." Barnum Brown died in 1963 at the age of 89. Fossils he discovered can still be seen in museums all over the world.

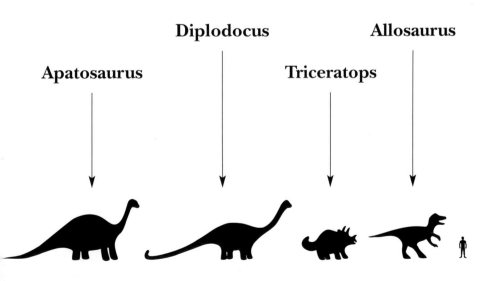

Diplodocus

Allosaurus

Apatosaurus

Triceratops

1 inch = 30 feet

Where Did Dinosaurs Go?

The study of fossils can answer many questions about dinosaurs. But there are many questions this study can't answer. One of the biggest questions is, where did all the dinosaurs go?

About 65 million years ago dinosaurs became extinct. They just disappeared from Earth. Paleontologists do not know exactly how the dinosaurs died. But they have many ideas.

Some believe that a rock from space hit Earth. This space rock is called a meteorite.

Some think the crash caused a huge dust cloud that blocked out the sunlight. Without sunlight, plants would have died. Without any food, the plant eaters would have died. Soon the meat eaters that ate the plant eaters would have died, too.

24

PLANT EATER

MEAT EATER

When plant life was destroyed, plant- and meat-eating dinosaurs became extinct, too.

The meteorite crash may have caused large waves. The crash may also have caused volcanoes to erupt. Experts think the dinosaurs could not have survived the results of these events.

Another idea is that Earth and its weather changed. The weather became colder. The dinosaurs could not adjust to the changed weather.

A Tyrannosaurus rex skeleton

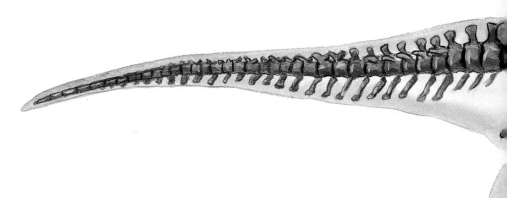

Others think that a disease might have killed the dinosaurs. Or perhaps early mammals ate too many of the dinosaurs' eggs.

Tyrannosaurus rex, the king of the dinosaurs, is extinct. But paleontologists are always finding new fossils. Sometimes these new fossils help answer questions. Sometimes they do not. Perhaps one day the mysteries of the "tyrant lizard king" and the other dinosaurs will be solved.

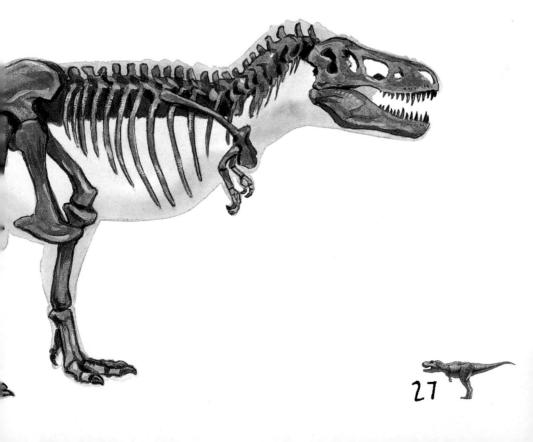

Dinosaur Dig

You can contact the following places for information on dinosaur digs.

1. Some local natural history museums, children's museums, and science museums sponsor real dinosaur digs all over the world. Sometimes they sponsor programs that let you look for fossils near your home. Some museums build their own digs inside the museum!

2. The Dinamation International Society gives information about dinosaurs. It offers digs throughout the United States, Mexico, Asia, South America, and Europe. For information call 1-800-DIG-DINO or write for a catalog to Director of Expeditions, Dinamation International Society, 550 Jurassic Court, Fruita, CO 81521. The society is also on the Web at www.Dinamation.org.

3. Museum of the Rockies Paleontology Field Program is run by the famous paleontologist Jack Horner. Write the museum at 406 W. Kagy, Bozeman, MT 59717 or call 1-406-994-6618.

4. Montana State University holds week-long digs near Havre, Montana. Their findings have been discussed in the book *Dinosaur Lives*, by Jack Horner.

Call 1-800-662-6132 extension 3716 or E-mail ClouseV@yahoo.com for information.

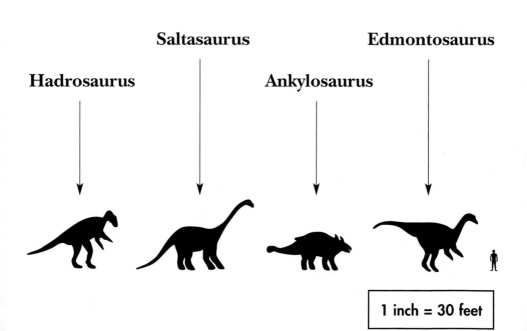

Hadrosaurus Saltasaurus Ankylosaurus Edmontosaurus

1 inch = 30 feet

Glossary

Cretaceous period (kreh-TAY-shus) The time period from 145 million to 65 million years ago

dinosaurs (DIE-nuh-sores) Land-dwelling reptiles that lived from 245 million to 65 million years ago

extinct (ex-TINKT) When groups die out they are said to be extinct.

fossil (FAH-sill) Remains of ancient life, such as a dinosaur bone or a footprint, or imprint, in a rock

mammals (MAM-ulls) Warm-blooded animals, usually with hair, that feed their young with milk

meteorite (MEE-tee-uh-rite) A rocky object from space that strikes Earth's surface. A meteorite can be a few inches or several miles wide.

paleontologist (pay-lee-on-TAH-luh-jist) A scientist who studies fossils

predator (PRED-uh-tur) A meat-eating animal that hunts and kills other animals for food

prey (PRAY) Animals eaten by predators

reptiles (REP-tiles) A group of air-breathing animals that lay eggs and usually have scaly skin

scavenger (SKAV-en-jer) An animal that eats dead animals left by predators

theory (THEE-uh-ree) Organized information that explains how we understand the world

Tyrannosaurus rex (tuh-ran-uh-SORE-us REX) One of the largest dinosaurs that ever lived

Index